MW00935579

MINDFUL MOMENTS

MINDFUL MOMENTS

A Collection of Life Wisdom, Black & White

ALICE INOUE

Copyright © 2015 Alice Inoue
All rights reserved.

ISBN: 1530217032
ISBN 13: 9781530217038
Library of Congress Control Number: 2015918518
CreateSpace Independent Publishing Platform
North Charleston, South Carolina

DEDICATION

To my readers, who inspire me to write every day.

SPECIAL
ACKNOWLEDGEMENT

Alan

You are an extraordinary guiding force in my life. Without you, I have no doubt that I would not be who I am today and would not be doing what I do. You have inspired me with your wisdom and have significantly influenced my path in life. You are an exceptional human being, and I'm thankful every day for your presence in my life.

ACKNOWLEDGMENTS

Ron Nagasawa – It is solely because of you that I have my two columns, and I love that you thought of the name *A Mindful Moment* for my MidWeek column. Words cannot properly express the depth of my gratitude for your friendship. Thank you for your belief in me.

Sarah Aschenbach – I am eternally thankful for all that that led me to find you in 2008 and that we could work on our sixth book together. I am convinced there is no one better in this world who can take what I write, understand what I'm trying to say, polish it up, and keep my voice woven in the way you do. You are amazing, Sarah.

Jason Lent –Had I been told when I first met you when you were seventeen that eighteen years later you would become such a big part of my life, I would never have believed it. I cherish our friendship, and I truly value your talent, creativity, and genius ideas. Thank you for designing this cover for me. I love it so much! www.lententerprises.com

Keli'i Grace – Your support is nothing short of amazing. Thank you for always so generously sharing your incredible talents to help me. I have great respect for all you do, and am thankful for your friendship. www.kaimediahawaii.com

Joe Gedeon – Thank you for coming forth to help me with the design layout. I'm so thankful for your support, and look forward to more great collaborations together! www.jpghawaii.com

SPECIAL THANKS

The Happiness U Team – Erin Ushijima, Valerie Moriwaki, Chad Sato, Shari Kimoto, David Marks, Judy Segawa, Karen Murashige, Marie-Jose Noyle, Kimi Morton, Gay Dochin, Mi Kosasa, Susan Toyama, Melanie Fox, Kay Yara, and Jamie Yoshida—without you there would be no Happiness U. And of course, my business coach, Anastacia Brice. I cannot imagine a life without you. You each have played a big part in my evolution towards all I do today.
Happiness U Members, Teachers and Supporters – There are too many of you to list, but you know who you are and I want you to know how much you mean to me.

Clients, Friends, and Family – You have enriched my life so fully and helped me in infinite ways throughout the years. Thank you. I am who I am because of you.

TABLE OF CONTENTS

INTRODUCTION

The fast pace of our lives in this new age of technology and ever-present distractions makes it increasingly difficult to slow down and be present as you go through the day. One day blurs into the next, and if you do not stay mindful of what is important, you can easily get ensnared in the hardships and complexities that life naturally brings and start thinking that difficulties are all there is to life.

When you develop a habit of focusing on the negatives more than on the positives, you may fail to see, or even to remember, that in every situation, there is another side, a positive side. We all need constructive reminders to keep us on track, and in my experience, the more the better. The Moments in this book were compiled to serve as a resource of positive reminders. It is my hope that they will help you when you need to see things from a fresh vantage point, or just when you need some inspiration.

When you open to seeing a different perspective, it's possible to shift your focus so significantly that, in one Aha moment, your perception of what is going on in your life can change, immediately helping you feel better. Less dramatic but still of value, you may simply change how you are experiencing something, and that can give you a more positive outlook to get you through the day just that much happier.

I compiled the Moments in this book from a column called "A Mindful Moment," which appears in Oahu's most-read weekly publication, *MidWeek.* Over a quarter million copies are delivered each week to nearly every Honolulu home. I am privileged to have the opportunity to write one Moment every week for the readers to ponder.

When the column first started in 2013, there was nothing like it in any of the major publications. After a few months, readers started writing in. Some said they find the Moments so useful that they clip them out and carry them around or display them on their desks. Soon, I received requests to compile them into a book—and now here I am with close to a hundred Moments to share with you!

The best way to incorporate the value in these Moments is to open the book at random to a page that *feels right* and read what your eye falls on. I'm pretty sure that almost every time, you will get a message that is exactly what you need to be aware of in that very moment. You may think of this as a coincidence, but I think of it as divine synchronicity.

My wish for you is that the words in this book help you at exactly the right time…in exactly the right way.

PART ONE
SIMPLE MOMENTS

Nothing happens to you
everything happens for **YOU.**
Your life has a purpose, and you are here for a reason.
No matter how you look, think or feel,
you are perfect in every way.
The more you focus on your own life,
the easier your life becomes.

Everything happens
in your life for a
reason—there are
no "accidents."

HAPPINESS

There really is no
"right" or wrong,"
only what's right
for you.

Everything you are doing or not doing in your life is serving a purpose.
Your own **intuition** is your
best source of **guidance.**
In every situation, there is always a bigger picture to consider.
YOU are responsible for your
own happiness.

©2013 Happiness U
YourHappinessU.com

YOU ARE HERE TO LOVE, NOT FIX

It's not your job to fix others and *make* them into the type of partner, child, husband, wife, boss, manager, co-worker, or employee that we want them to be—no matter how *off* or wrong you think they are. You are here to appreciate them, learn from them, share perspectives with them, love them, and communicate with them, and inspire them to be the most authentic person they can be. Love people for who they are, not for who you want them to be. It's not always easy to do this, but it's good to keep in mind.

KNOW WHAT'S IMPORTANT TO YOU

When you don't know what you want, others will gladly determine that for you based on what *they* want. That's why it's important to know yourself and know what's important to you. When you are moving in the direction you have chosen, it's much easier to embrace the challenges than when you are doing what someone else wants you to do. The pain of regret is always greater than the pain of discipline. Don't waste your life doing what someone else wants you to do and suppressing the magnificence of your own potential. It's not worth it in the long run.

REMEMBER WHAT WENT RIGHT

At the end of the day, it's easy to remember what went wrong and what didn't go according to plan, but also remember to affirm what has gone right.

- Where were you successful?
- Where were you productive?
- Where were you heard?
- Where did you make a difference?

Take this opportunity to end your day on a balanced note. Only when you recognize and find meaning in both your positives and your negatives can true gratitude emerge and find its place in your heart.

ACKNOWLEDGE THE GIFTS YOU'VE BEEN GIVEN

If you gave someone a gift and they tossed it aside without acknowledgement or thanks, would you want to give them another gift? Probably not. In the same way, this is how the universe responds when you don't acknowledge the gifts that you have been given. The universe presents gifts where they are most appreciated. It's wise to remember that we humans are built in line with universal principles, and the universe operates in exactly the same way, too. If you are not appreciative now for who you are and what you have, why would the universe give you more? The more appreciative you are today, the more you will have to appreciate tomorrow.

AFFIRM YOUR GOODNESS

Today and every day, take the time to acknowledge and affirm the good things you see in yourself. The more you appreciate, love, and accept yourself for exactly who you are, the more powerful the love you have to give. The magic happens when you feel the magnitude of that love come back to you. Let the love you feel around you be a reminder of the love you have within you. What we see and experience is always a reflection of who we think we are.

APPRECIATE TODAY

BECAUSE UNLIKE MOST
JOURNEYS, GETTING TO
THE END IS NOT THE
GOAL OF YOUR LIFE.

YourHappinessU.com

HOW WILL YOU SPEND TODAY?

How are you using your day, today? What you do every day is important because you are exchanging your life for it. When tomorrow arrives, today will be gone forever. So be present, enjoy the day, do something that you find joyful, share your love, open your heart, and affirm that any and all synchronicities that you experience are "messages," telling you that all is well and you are on the right path. A synchronicity can be anything you notice that seems "divine." It might be a friend calling just when you were thinking of them or running into a person you've been meaning to get in touch with in a random place. Let the essence of the moment seed something positive for you.

NO MATTER WHAT, YOU CANNOT FAIL

Why can't you fail? Because when you are on the path that is right for you and are truly inspired, you won't give up. It may be difficult and challenging, and you may fall again and again, but you will always get back up and keep going. When you do fall, when you feel, "That's it. I'm done," make sure you don't label it as a failure. See it as the gift it is. Why? Your decision to change direction shows that what you were going after is no longer important to you. It's the perfect feedback mechanism. We never give up on the things that truly matter to us. We do, however, give up on the things that don't.

MAGNETIZE OPPORTUNITIES TOWARDS YOU

Is your life filled with results or excuses? If you want results, you have to take responsibility for your life and your outlook and position yourself in such a way that you consistently look for advantages instead of disadvantages. By doing so, you will inevitably pull opportunities and synchronicities into your path. People, money, resources, and opportunities are drawn towards positive energy, optimism, and certainty. If you feel that your life is less than optimal, take a moment to reset your focus. Place your attention on the area of your life in which you feel hope, natural enthusiasm, and confidence. The change in focus will shift your overall energy so you can begin drawing opportunities into your life effortlessly.

AFFIRM YOUR DREAMS

Take time to positively affirm your dreams, visions, and heartfelt goals. Do not bury them because of others' opinions, perceptions, and judgments. Whenever you subordinate your dreams and desires to someone else, you are moving against your intrinsic nature, which is to radiate, expand, and grow.

EMBRACE DISCOMFORT TODAY

Don't allow feeling uncomfortable to stop you from doing or saying what you want. Face the discomfort, embrace it, and do what you know inside is right for you. Until you do, you will continue to attract lessons into your life. For example, if you feel too uncomfortable to say no to someone who doesn't appreciate your time or energy, you are neglecting your truth. Saying yes when you want to say no will attract increasingly greater frustration until you finally get the "lesson" and learn to say no. Embrace discomfort today to avoid frustrations tomorrow.

The Balance of Life

There will always always always be something to be grateful for.

There will always always always be something you wish didn't exist.

#PerfectBalance
#AcceptLifeAsItIs

YourHappinessU.com

LOOK FOR THE HIDDEN

If you are under a lot of pressure, take a deep breath, slow down, and look around. The hardships and frustrating events in life can be easier to manage if you consciously choose to see the secondary gains, which are not as obvious. Every challenge in your life has a hidden benefit. Don't stay in a state of frustration and blame. Take the time to look for the benefit or you will lose out.

THINGS ARE FALLING TOGETHER

I know at times it may feel like your life is falling apart, but trust that, actually, it is falling together in perfect alignment. It only feels scary because you haven't seen the final manifestation of what is yet to unfold for you;

you are blind to how your life is going to take shape. When it does take shape, though, everything that is happening now will make sense, and you will realize why you had to go through this experience. Your current fears are an incomplete view of what is happening. Thus, live fully! Walk with certainty, knowing that each and every day you are moving towards more of who you are and away from who you are not, leading to balance and joy in your heart.

WHAT ARE YOU CREATING?

You are the creator of your own reality. This is why it is important to pay careful attention to what you are creating and how you are creating it. Did you know that everything you say to yourself—silently or aloud, good or bad, true or false—is imprinted on your conscious and subconscious mind and becomes part of what you believe? It's true! Is it time for you to develop a new language for your self-talk?

Once you believe what you are saying, you start living out these state-ments, regardless of whether doing so is taking you where you want to go or not. Ask yourself: is it time for me to develop a new language and imprint my mind with statements that get me on track instead of using ones that continually hold me back?

THINGS ARE COMING TOGETHER

Do you realize that, at this very moment, things are coming together for you in ways that are not yet apparent to you? As your inspired visions are becoming reality, a lot goes on behind the scenes. So, if you are frus-trated or if things are not happening as soon as you'd like, stop and take note of what *is* happening. Notice all the synchronicities you actually experience each day. You know that some things *do* happen at the right time and *do* come together in the right way. Even if small, these are all signs to let you know that you are on the right track. Start by affirming the small things, and before you know it, the big things will become a part of your reality.

ACCEPT THE NEGATIVE

Being positive all the time does not equate to being happy. In fact, trying to be positive all the time will take you away from ease in your heart and balance in your life, which is what most of us are trying to achieve. Negativity is part of life. Don't fight it, judge it, or resist it. Thinking negative is not bad; it's part of bringing forth the balance. So, when it comes to obstacles, negative thoughts, and challenges, remember that what you resist will persist and what you embrace will dissipate. Accept the negative so you can get on with your life.

Your heart has a vision.
LET IT BEAT
OUT LOUD!

HAPPINESS
YourHappinessU.com

WIDEN YOUR PERSPECTIVE

If you are currently experiencing emotional pain over a situation in your life, it's because your perspective is too narrow, and you have yet to experience all the benefits and gifts that will emerge from this situation. We are living in a time of great change. If you are going through changes and can't see the light at the end of the tunnel, yet, I want to affirm that you are in the right place. There is no mistake. You will grow through this. Things will get better. Just take one step at a time and trust in the bigger picture you have yet to see in which your heart is at ease.

TWO SIDES OF THE COIN

Life is a unique mix of happy and sad, good and bad, easy and tough, and simple and rough. The secret to balancing out erratic emotional swings is to stay ever mindful of the fact that one polarity does not exist without the other, and that opposites are simply two sides of the same coin. So, when you are experiencing something that feels bad or sad, be aware that good and happy also exist in that moment—just behind a veil in your awareness. Embracing this mindset will open your heart in new ways, revealing to you a clear path towards your greatest potential.

EMBRACE THE PRESENT

It's time to fully embrace the present and be bolder than you have ever dared. Today, find meaning in your challenges; use them as fuel for your inspiration. Rise up each day and pursue life with a renewed focus. Feel your pains deeply while fully embracing your challenges, and just as day follows night, your life will take flight again as a greater and even more meaningful purpose emerges.

SHIFT YOUR FOCUS

If you are facing challenges that you feel you cannot control, you probably feel down when you think about them. This is the time to use your ability to shift your focus at will, and turn it to the power of *I am*. Instead of saying, "I am stressed, I am sad, I am angry," begin affirming, "*I am* doing the best I can. *I am* seeing more support come forth. *I am* finding new ways to cope. *I am* in charge of how I look at this situation. *I am* blessed in other ways." The word *affirmation* means *to make firm in your mind.* What is a positive *I am* that you can affirm today?

OUR GROWTH IS THE PURPOSE OF LIFE

Life is not meant to get easier. We are meant to grow into our greatest power, strength, and authenticity. The degree to which you wish your life was easier is the degree to which your challenges will feel overwhelming. It helps to remember that wishing life's challenges to go away is absolutely no help. What helps is to look for how the challenges you have are helping you to grow and get stronger. If life feels tough right now, remember: what you resist persists, and what you embrace dissipates.

The Universe is a great teacher and gives us exactly what we need to grow and evolve to our fullest potential.

LOOK FOR LOVE AND WONDER

When all else fails and life feels miserable, look for love and wonder. The more you look for it, the more you will find. Start small. Appreciate things like your favorite drink, your best friend's loving voice, your child's smile, or your pet's unconditional joy at seeing you. Perhaps, take notice of the beauty of sunshine and moonlight. Be present with your body and witness its desire to stay alive with every inhale and exhale, and with every beat of your heart. Focus on that which is stable and certain in your life, and slowly but surely, just as day follows night, the dawn of a new awareness will emerge. Love and joy are always present. Sometimes, they're just hidden behind the veils of our misery.

BE PRESENT TO ENJOY YOUR DAY

How are you using this moment? What you do in every moment is important because you are exchanging your life for it! When tomorrow arrives, today will be gone forever. Be present, enjoy the day as it unfolds, create something unique, share your love, and open your heart. Let the essence of the moment seed something amazing for you.

CULTIVATE GRATITUDE FOR EVERYTHING

Cultivate the habit of being grateful for every good thing that comes to you, and not only that, but for every challenge and unexpected happening that throws you off-course. Since all things that happen in life contribute to your advancement and growth, it is wise to include all things in your gratitude. Honoring the full spectrum of all that happens in your life brings greater balance to the core of your existence. What challenge can you find benefit in and be thankful for today?

GIVE MORE TO RECEIVE MORE

If you would like to give more, make it a point to receive more. This may sound strange, but there must be an even exchange of energy in all you do in order for you to be truly balanced. Giving is *not* better than "receiving," as many of us were raised to think. They are complementary opposites. If you are always giving and don't allow yourself to receive, you will not only drain your energy, but you will proportionately limit what you are ultimately able to give. Ask yourself, "Where can I be more open to receiving today so that I have more to give tomorrow?" As you allow yourself to receive more, you raise your ability to give more.

BE INSPIRED BY WHAT YOU DO

If you want to be an entrepreneur, make sure you do it because you are inspired by the service or products you plan to offer. If you start your own business simply for the pursuit of a financial gain, you won't weather the inevitable challenges gracefully, nor will you embrace the natural ups and downs that are part of the entrepreneurial path.

As a result, sooner or later, you will burn yourself out and be unsuccessful in growing your business. Being inspired by what you do and expecting to work hard to continually refine it are secrets to entrepreneurial success. We only refine what we deem to be valuable.

ACKNOWLEDGE YOUR ACCOMPLISHMENTS

At the end of each day, reflect on what you accomplished and achieved. We naturally tend to focus on what we didn't do and beat ourselves up for not achieving it. If you take time to acknowledge what you did accomplish and spend a moment thinking about what you are grateful for, you will have more to be thankful for tomorrow.

LOVE AND APPRECIATE YOURSELF

Today and every day, take time to affirm the positive things about you. The more you appreciate, love, and accept yourself for exactly who you are, the more powerful the love you have to give. Let the love you feel around you remind you of the love you have within you. What you see and experience are always reflections of who you think you are.

BE A CREATURE OF GOOD HABITS

We are all creatures of habit, and it's easy to fall into stress-producing habits unconsciously. Some of these habits may be things you don't even like to do in the first place! Today, consciously notice how you spend your time and objectively determine which habits are productive and which are not. When you see a habit or become aware of a daily routine that decreases your productivity or sabotages your well-being, make a commitment to change it. Tomorrow, all you need to do is to change *one thing*. Don't try to revamp all your bad habits at once. Just commit to one thing, and you will have a good chance of being successful.

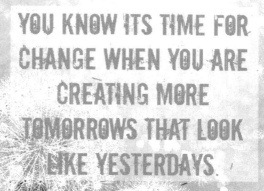

YOU KNOW ITS TIME FOR CHANGE WHEN YOU ARE CREATING MORE TOMORROWS THAT LOOK LIKE YESTERDAYS.

HAPPINESS

YourHappinessU.com

HOW TO FEEL GOOD

If you want to feel good more of the time rather than less of the time, affirm things that are true for you. Rather than running a monologue about how stressed you are, how unhealthy you are, or how unfocused you are, start affirming your truths: "I am doing my best. I am blessed with a job. I am a caring person." Only you can make a lasting change in how you feel about yourself, and this, in turn, can positively affect others.

LIVE CONSCIOUSLY

Let's strive to live consciously in each moment—with every decision, every greeting, every conversation, and every bite of every meal. Remember, it serves no purpose to look back and regret anything in your life. Yesterday is gone. Knowing this, reframe your thoughts so that the words you speak reflect the best of who you are today. Yesterday is no longer, so live your life fully present with every breath you take, as what you say and think today forms the foundation for all your tomorrows.

WHAT HAS GONE RIGHT

It's easy to remember what went wrong, but remember to also affirm what has gone right.

- Where were you successful?
- Where were you productive?
- Where were you heard?
- Where did you make a difference?

Only when you bring awareness to both the positive and the negatives in your life can true gratitude emerge and find its place in your heart.

THE CHOICE IS YOURS

Ultimately, you can choose to see the challenges in your life as happening *to* you or happening *for* you. For example, are your financial challenges helping you to be more resourceful? Are you experiencing health challenges so you can find new ways to live? Did a relationship end, giving you more time to focus on yourself? Look for the gift of a new perspective in the hidden benefits of your challenges, and self-create greater peace of mind.

Decide what YOU want (or someone else will).

"I KNOW WHAT I WANT FACE"

YourHappinessU.com

YOU ARE IN THE RIGHT PLACE

You are exactly where you need to be. The only thing that stops you from appreciating where you are is the idea that you should be somewhere else. In fact, you may be overlooking multiple gains and gifts in your current experience. Affirm the positive daily so you can let go of the mindset and struggle of believing you need to be somewhere else. You really are in the right place—and in the right life.

ON HELPING OTHERS

Many people say they want to help others, and one of the many ways to do this is to focus on yourself. If this sounds backwards or selfish to you, look at it this way: When you invest time in yourself and grow as a human being, you raise your self-worth, and by doing so, your value to others increases proportionately. When you value yourself, others find even more value in what you have to give. Truly, this is a win-win.

WHAT DOES IT MEAN TO BE SELF-EMPOWERED?

We hear the word *self-empowerment* a lot these days. What does it mean? To me, it means *acting* from inner conviction rather *reacting* due to external pressures. Self-empowerment means being inspired by an inner vision and having the courage to listen your inner voice rather than to the voices and opinions of others in your environment. I believe that self-empowered people share who they are authentically with others and don't imitate or envy anyone. Instead, they embrace love, growth, and challenge simultaneously. Now, what does self-empowerment mean to you?

IT'S WORTH THE OPPOSITION

Many people don't do what they really want to do because they fear rejection or opposition by family, friends, or the groups they associate with. If you are not living the life you want, don't forget that others will come and go, but only you will be with yourself forever. While it may be true that the more you live out your true desires, the more opposition you will have to deal with, don't forget, the flip side is that you will feel happier and your life will take on extraordinary meaning. Live your own life, and allow others to live theirs.

FORGET THE SHOULDS

Are there things you want to do that you just can't seem to get around to doing? Do you often think that you *should* eat healthier, *should* save more money, *should* find another job, or *should* keep your house neater? If so, let go of these negative *shoulds* to conserve your precious energy. Accept that you will do those things if, and when, you see a true benefit to doing so. Have you noticed that you always have the time, energy, and money to do the things you *really* want to do?

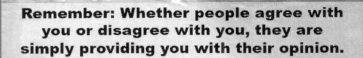

Remember: Whether people agree with you or disagree with you, they are simply providing you with their opinion.

THE VALUE OF YOU

When you do a service for others in business and charge less than you feel you really deserve (thinking that getting "some" money is better than none at all), you not only instantly reduce your self-value, dampen your spirits, and lower your standards, you also create a weak link in your business. This weak link slows your growth and supports inefficiency, which leads to a loss of overall effectiveness. To master your business (and your life), make sure that you are inspired by what you do and value your time and energy. How efficient and effective are you at doing what is truly important to you? Make an "even exchange of energy" the standard by which you operate, and your business will thrive.

SEE THE HIDDEN GIFTS

Every single challenge in life happens so that we can experience a new level of love and understanding of the people in our lives and the world we live in. The moment we embrace the pain and see the hidden gift, we awaken to new truths that guide us. When we can accept *what is*, we move through our hardships and open the path for blessings to unfold gracefully and in unprecedented ways.

GET OUT OF YOUR TRAP

Are you stuck in a rut? Do you feel that, as busy as you are, your life is strangely stagnant? If so, it's simply because you are not allowing yourself to go after what you really want. You may not even know what you want because you've been repressing your true desires for so long that you're trapped in a routine that lacks meaning for you. The first step is to ask yourself what you *really* want and identify the fears that are holding you back. Awareness is the key to freedom from your self-imposed stagnation.

YOU ARE THE AUTHOR OF YOUR LIFE

What is the content of your internal dialogue? Why do I ask? Because what you say to yourself has a huge impact on what happens to you and on the circumstances you draw into your experience. You are the author of your own life. Always keep this truth at the top of your mind. You write the chapters with every thought you have and every word you say. I truly believe that the more respect, love, and appreciation you have for yourself, the more successful you will be in every area of your life.

Sometimes its as easy as making a different choice.

YourHappinessU.com

#WhenInDoubtChooseLove

LIFE IS UNEXPLAINABLE

Life is filled with situations and circumstances that are unexplainable. Some bring joy to your heart, and others bring deep pain. If you are in a challenging situation and wonder how you can get through another moment, let alone another day, the way to move through it faster is to work towards embracing *what is*. You can make positive progress only when you stop wishing your life was something it isn't and embrace it for what it is.

WHAT DO YOU WANT?

The more specific you get about what you want, the more likely you are to bring it to you. There is a big difference between saying to yourself, "I want more money," and "I want to find work that I love that pays me

$5,000 per month." There is a big difference between saying, "I want better health," and "I want to eat a healthy breakfast to improve my health." One kind of self-talk is vague and unbalanced, and the other is specific, inspiring, and complete. Get specific if you want specific results.

YOU MAKE A DIFFERENCE

Remember, every single thing you do and say makes a difference. You are an intricate, and vital part of this world, so do not discount the profound effect that you have on the people around you, as well as on people you don't even know. If you say something that helps someone, and they help another with those same words, you have made a difference. What do you want to say and do today to initiate a ripple of positivity?

YOU ARE MAGNIFICENT

You are a magnificent human being. You are a vital part of this amazing world we live in, and your presence on this planet makes a difference to so many. Know that you are loved, appreciated, and cared for. If you need proof, reach out to others with words of love and appreciation today, and see what happens to confirm this. The essence of who you are is exceptional, inimitable, and irreplaceable.

DON'T BETRAY YOURSELF TO PLEASE OTHERS

Give yourself permission to fully live *your* life. It's easy to lose your center when you get caught up in doing what others think is best for you.

Practice being "self-centered"—not in an egotistical way, but in a loving way. Only from a place of centeredness can you make the best decisions for you and provide the best service to others. Is it time for you stand closer to the center of your own being and stop betraying yourself to please others?

SOMEDAYS YOU JUST GOTTA CREATE YOUR OWN SUNSHINE

HAPPINESS
YourHappinessU.com

HUMILITY IS ESSENTIAL

The practice of humility is an essential daily exercise. When you show humility, you inspire silent respect from others. Humility not only fosters personal growth, but it keeps your ego from over-reacting, which prevents arguments and curbs your tendency to be defensive. Humility reminds us that we still have a lot to learn. No matter how much we think we know, when compared to the magnificence of the universe we live in, what we know is really only a drop in the universal ocean of life.

LOVE YOURSELF

When you think you need to be a more perfect version of you, you close down to opportunities. Embrace your value, and you will automatically receive more blessings than ever before. You transform your life when you appreciate yourself for who you are instead of depreciating yourself for not being someone you think you should be. Your conscious focus on your assets has the power to bring more positive experiences into your life. The most important relationship is the one that you have with you. If you get this, you get life.

YOU ARE IMPORTANT

Have you ever noticed that you lose your sense of self when you see someone as better than you in some way? When you think another's opinion is more important than yours, you feel the pain of rejection, minimize yourself relative to them, and start sacrificing your own needs and desires to please them. Don't lose yourself by trying to please those you think are more important than you. Remember, *you* are just as important, and you are not to be minimized. Honor your true and radiant self.

THE BEAUTY OF WHAT *IS*

Have you ever thought, "My life is not supposed to be like this?" While it's natural to complain during challenging times, if you get all wrapped up in how your life is *supposed* to be, you'll miss the beauty of what it actually is. Do you wish your ex never existed? If not, you wouldn't have your children. Do you wish your work was more meaningful? Without it, you would have never met your great co-worker friends. The beauty of life is always there when we take the time to look for it.

MONITOR YOUR THOUGHTS

Make it a point to consistently monitor your thoughts, because what you think about, you bring about. If you regularly think about how much you dislike your life, your job, your relationships, your looks, your predicament, and so forth, the people you encounter on a daily basis will sense this and may shut down to you or even withhold opportunities as a result. Affirm daily the things you *do* like and the things that *are* going well so what you are thinking about becomes the reality you are projecting.

REFLECTIONS

When I reflect upon my life, I can see that literally everything I have ever experienced has served me to perfection and added infinite value to my life. The disappointments, shattered dreams, and betrayals have helped me to grow in ways that have led me to my greatest joys and accomplishments, as it has for you. Because of this, it's almost impossible not to feel humbled by the intelligence that governs this universe and blown away by the divine order of synchronicities that brings the people, circumstances, and situations to you in exactly the way you need.

EXPAND YOUR THINKING

I invite you to expand your thinking beyond what you perceive is possible for your life. No matter how complex and challenging your life is, or how unique your situation, there is a way to move through it, and the reality that you have created for yourself has to change in order for you to change. If you spend more time focusing on your vision than you do on complaining about the obstacles in the way, you'll be where you want to be before you know it.

CREATE EASE

At the end of each day, take a "mindful moment" to be thankful for all that transpired today—both the good and not so good. I invite you to create more ease for yourself by making a commitment to stop fighting what you can't change, which includes others and things you can't control. Doing this will profoundly change your experience. Just focus on what you want instead of on the obstacles you are currently facing, and watch things unfold with greater ease.

BUSINESS SUCCESS SECRET

If you are an entrepreneur or business owner, it's important not to get so wrapped up in the day-to-day running of the business that you stop learning and growing. I've noticed that if the rate of change outside your business is greater than the rate of change inside your business, things get very hard, very quickly. You can easily start losing your edge and see diminished engagement. Take the time to nurture your genius, grow your brilliance, and invest in your spirit daily. Your ultimate business success depends on it.

A WEEK OF RESULTS

Do you want this week to be filled with results or excuses? If you want results, make a commitment right now to consistently look for the advantages in every situation, and not the disadvantages. By doing so, you will inevitably magnetize unexpected opportunities and synchronicities into your path. People, money, and resources are compellingly drawn toward positive energy, optimism, and certainty. If you place your attention on where you have hope, natural enthusiasm, and confidence, you will start the process of drawing an abundance of opportunities to you. Right now, think of one advantage of a current challenge, and you will be on your way to manifesting positive results.

Find time for what makes you happy to be alive.

#LifeWithoutMeaningSucks

YourHappinessU.com

TRUE GRATITUDE

If you make it a habit to count your blessings, you will attract more blessings and experience more meaning in your life than those who don't. It may seem too easy, yet counting your blessings has the power to change your life. Many think they are grateful when, actually, they are confusing gratitude with elation. Elation is a temporary moment of happiness you may feel intermittently, whereas true gratitude is a quiet state of inner calm in which you feel truly thankful as you recognize the divine order and perfection of your life.

APPRECIATE YOURSELF AND OTHERS

When you are infatuated with someone, you tend to idolize them and minimize yourself in comparison to them because you think they have something you don't. Consciously or subconsciously, you tend to subordinate yourself to them. On the other hand, when you resent someone, you put them down, see only their down side, and want to change them. The balanced, wise, and mindful way is to appreciate ourselves for who we are and others exactly as they are.

LOVING YOURSELF IS A SERVICE TO OTHERS

People often tell me that they want to help others and be a good role model. One way to help others is to love, respect, and accept yourself for who you are. If you don't value yourself, why would anyone value you? If you don't enjoy yourself, how can anyone enjoy you? Accepting ourselves for who we are is one of the hardest things to do. As unlikely as it may sound, you can actually help others and inspire them by simply living a life of self-acceptance. It always inspires me to see people who accept themselves as they are.

WHAT SOMEONE ELSE THINKS IS ONLY AN OPINION

Why do you feel so awful when someone puts you down? Whether people agree with you or disagree, they are simply giving you their opinion. You feel bad about it only if you think the same way.

WE ARE BORN TO GROW

Do you ever wake up wanting to shrink and wanting to do less, be less, and amount to less? No! Sometimes when you feel challenged, you may have these thoughts, but it is not part of your intrinsic nature to want less or be less. We human beings are in a constant state of expansion, and the things we think are missing are the very things that drive us towards our greatest growth.

SHINE IN YOUR OWN WAY

If you get upset when others criticize you, label you, or try to make you into someone you are not, after a while you might start thinking that something is wrong with you. If this is true for you, don't believe your thoughts. The truth is that you are a unique individual; there is nothing *wrong* with you. Others (and maybe you) simply do not appreciate the beauty and the radiance deep within you. Just keep your focus on what is ultimately most inspiring to you and shine in your own authentic way.

SLEEP WITH GRATITUDE

Tonight, as you lie in bed, think back over your day. Make it a point to remember those who have helped you. See them in your mind's eye and thank them for their support. Next, think of everyone who has challenged you. See them in your mind's eye and thank them for challenging you. Why? Because we grow on the edges of challenge and support, so everyone in your life is helping you grow. Make this a nightly practice, and you will wake up with a more balanced outlook and a more open heart.

INSPIRE OTHERS BY LOVING WHO YOU ARE

People often think they need to attain some level of perfection or meet some standard in order to be an inspiration to others. In fact, accepting yourself for who you are and *as you are* is inspiring in and of itself. In which areas of your life do you feel confident? How can you change your view of yourself to reflect greater acceptance instead of greater disappointment? Find ways to love who you are. It is infinitely more inspiring than beating up on yourself for not being at some ideal level of perfection or achievement.

YOUR TIME IS IMPORTANT

Anything you do takes time, and your time is valuable. To make the most of your time, every day make it a point to prioritize how you want to spend it. Others may want your time and may think you are being rude when you say no. Caution: If you don't firmly decide how *you* want to use your time, others gladly will, and this will lead to resentment in the long term and create a time shortage for you in the short term. If you are feeling overwhelmed, it would be wise to raise your standards about time.

BE A QUALITY LISTENER

It is wise to be mindful that there are endless perspectives and opinions about everything in this world, and yours is simply one of them. Often, we want to be right and feel we need to push our opinions on others, but is that really the best approach to interacting with people we care about? Listening to other people's viewpoints expands your awareness. Being a good listener pays off, and truly listening before you speak opens the door to heartfelt communication.

Be
ungrateful

Why would the Universe
give you anything if you
don't even appreciate
what you have?

YourHappinessU.com

APPRECIATE WHERE YOU ARE

It's natural to think that when you get something that you don't currently have, life will get easier or better. "When I lose ten pounds, my life will be better," or "When I have more money, life will be easier," but all it really does is transform the challenges of your current experience into new forms. Have you noticed in the past, that when you get what you imagine you wanted, there was a twist to it or something unexpected happened? Go for what you want, but just remember to appreciate where you are, and not get caught up in a fantasy about the future.

FIND THE BALANCE

Strive to find balance each day. Right smack in the middle between positive and negative emotions, between good and bad feelings, and between infatuation and resentment is the core of the human experience…and it is nothing other than love. So instead of wishing for a life with "perfect" partners, friend, spouses, children, boss, employees, appreciate everyone in your life for what they bring to you. Without their contribution, your life wouldn't be the same.

WHAT IS MOST IMPORTANT?

Take the time to identify what is truly most valuable to you, and give yourself permission to start letting go of your low priorities. When you concentrate on your higher priorities, you begin the process of mastering your life. Why do this? Because at the end of your life, you want to be able to say that you did everything you could with everything you were given. You are an extraordinary human being, and you have what it takes to be successful. So, do what is meaningful to you. Put your focus on what is valuable to you and give yourself permission to shine.

IT'S ABOUT YOU

Sometimes the people you complain about—you know, the ones that stress you out and create obstacles—are actually assisting you the most. Why? Because they force you to face what in *you* is holding you back from achieving your goals. So, instead of lamenting about these irritating people, ask yourself some questions:

- Do you need to refocus on what's important?
- Do you need to get over the need to please others?
- Do you need to let go of judgments?
- Do you need to change who you hang out with?

Remember, it's not about them. It always is about you, and it always will be about you.

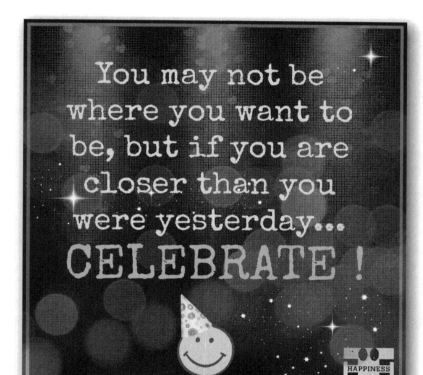

ACCEPT YOURSELF AS YOU ARE

If you love and accept yourself, it is much easier to love and accept others. This is because everything you see in others mirrors what is in you. Whenever you put someone down or get irritated with a certain trait in them, it's actually because you have the same trait within you, and you either don't want to admit it, think you don't have it, want to get rid of it, suppress the expression of it, or judge it to be wrong. Make life easier for yourself: instead of trying to change others, which never works, work on accepting yourself for all that you are and watch how it almost magically stops the other person from getting on your last nerve.

AN IMPORTANT REMINDER

Your time and energy are yours. It's easy to forget sometimes that you are the 100 percent full owner of them. As an owner of your time, this means you can choose how you want to spend your time and energy, because they are yours to spend. If there are people in your life who expect you to freely give them your time or energy without paying for it with some form of value or an equal exchange of energy (money, appreciation, reciprocation, etc.), then it's either time to either start saying No or start making plans to clear out your "people clutter." Is it time to reclaim your time and energy so you can do with it as *you* please?

PART TWO

MOMENTS FOR REFLECTION

HAVE YOU BEEN PROCRASTINATING?

When you are beating yourself up for not doing what you think you should be doing, use this affirmation: "I always get done what I need to get done when the time is right." Whenever you procrastinate or feel unproductive, you are forgetting that you are, in fact, doing what you want to do or need to do in that moment.

Remember, it's okay to be "inspired" to be lazy! It's not natural to always be productive. It truly is all about balance. As soon as you embrace this, it won't be long before you will feel inspired to do something else. Just as there is an exhale for every inhale, so also do you need an even balance of doing "nothing" and being active. Do both this weekend with consciousness, and let's have gratitude in our hearts for simply being alive!

FIND YOUR BALANCE

Strive for balance every day. Right smack in the middle between positive and negative emotions, between good and bad feelings, and between infatuation and resentment is the core of the human experience—and it is nothing other than love. So, instead of wishing for a life with perfect partners, friends, spouses, children, bosses, and employees, appreciate everyone in your life for what they bring to you. Without their contribution, your life would not be the same.

In the same way, you'll find that love exists exactly in the middle between your pains and pleasures, your challenges and joys, and your ups and downs. When "Debbie Downer" comes along to burst your bubble, she is there to help you find balance. When "Positive Penny" comes along to lift your spirits, she is there to help you find balance. Love is there when you accept life for what it is and stand in the center of the core of your existence.

FACEBOOK REALITY IS NOT LIFE'S REALITY

Do you ever look at other people's pictures on Facebook and think how perfect their lives look without being conscious that you are seeing only a curated stream of the happiest and most successful highlights? It's easy to feel like you are falling short somehow in the happiness or fun department.

I'm sure that, at times, Facebook has caused millions of people to feel inadequate when they compare their very real two-sided lives to the mythical one-sided lives they see online. It's easy to fall into thinking that a perfect life means having all of the good and none of the bad, and being happy and never sad.

The word *perfect* actually means *complete in all respects.* So, embrace your life exactly as it is without comparing or contrasting. Remember, no matter what is presented publicly, there is always another side that exists privately, because it is impossible for one side to exist without the other in the two-sided reality of life.

DO NEGATIVE PEOPLE BOTHER YOU?

The more you judge certain people in your life as negative, with the judgment that negativity is bad, the more their negativity will bother you. Focusing on it and contrasting their attitude to your perceived positivity, with the judgment that you are right, makes it harder to just get on with your day. As you constantly point out the negative in them to yourself and others, you are forgetting that you are also being and doing the very thing that bothers you about them! The best thing to do is to accept negative people for who they are and focus on what is important to you.

YOU ARE UTTERLY FREE

How you forgotten how powerful you are? Do you know you are free to create anything you want in your life? Nothing feels worse than the perception that you are powerless and unable to get your life going in certain areas. Although you may feel trapped by certain circumstances in your life, in reality you are utterly free.

How so? You are free to change your thoughts about your situation. Remember, energy responds to the direction of your thoughts, so don't keep recreating the same energy by focusing on areas in which you are struggling. Only when you bring your awareness to the positives in a negative situation can you neutralize your resistance—and that is when the road out magically appears. Your life is not stuck. You are just stuck in thinking the same thoughts over and over again.

Life is a Gift.

BE PRESENT

STAY FOCUSED AND BE PRODUCTIVE

We often have so many stresses and distractions throughout the day that it can be difficult to stay focused. When a lot of tasks are running around in my head, it helps me to put those things down on paper and check them off as I work. A list serves as a reminder of what I want to accomplish and helps keep me focused.

Anything you can put down on paper will reduce your stress and add to your success. There is something magical and inspiring when you can check off what you have done, item by item. Here is my personal secret: When I sit down to write my list, I write down things I have already done and check them off right then! Feeling productive is one of the best feelings in the world.

ARE YOU FEELING UNPRODUCTIVE?

Have you noticed that when you are busy and have a deadline, you get more done in less time than when you don't have a deadline? The more focused you are and the longer you can maintain it, the more productive you are and the faster your accomplishments accumulate. Conversely, the more time you spend on low-priority actions, worry, doubt, and fear, the less you get done. If you are feeling unproductive, look at what you are doing and delegate and/or refocus. Do things that inspire you to fulfill your vision, and you won't have time for the self-doubt and distractions that block them.

What can you learn from this? Since you always get your have-to-dos done anyway, you can give yourself *full* permission to do what you want to do in the moment. When you are in the moment, doing what you are doing, but simultaneously beating yourself up for not doing what you think you *should* be doing, you are splitting your energy, creating drag, and dampening your spirit. It's counter-productive! When you give yourself up to the moment, no matter what you are doing, you become alive, focused, and inspired, which is an awesome state of mind to be in.

Here is your new affirmation for times when you are judging yourself as unproductive: "I always get done what I need to get done when the time is right. I am in the right place, at the right time, doing the right thing."

COMPARE YOURSELF TO WHAT'S REAL

The universal Law of Relativity has many applications. For example, you can apply it when you don't feel good about your physical appearance. We tend to beat ourselves up for how we look because we have unrealistic expectations that were seeded from what we have seen for years in the media and magazines as to what beauty is. Anytime you have negative feelings about your body shape, weight, age, or a specific body part, it's because you are comparing yourself to what you think you *should* look like.

This is where the Law of Relativity can be helpful. It states "nothing is good or bad, big or small, until you relate it to something else." Your body appearance just *is*—until you start making comparisons. Remember this law so you can begin to accept yourself as you are. Instead of comparing yourself to a fantasy in your head, notice the real people you see around you. You will feel so much better and be closer to accepting yourself just as you are. Everything truly is relative.

ARE YOU GIVING IT AWAY FOR FREE?

During my college days, I often heard guys talking about the girls who "slept around," describing them as being "cheap," calling them "easy," and devaluing them. Feeling devalued, no doubt the girls devalued themselves.

We all devalue ourselves to some extent, especially in areas where we feel less confident and don't own our power or see our intrinsic value. And whenever you consistently do not operate according to the standard of an even exchange of value, you automatically decrease the value of what you offer.

To whom do you subordinate yourself and tend to over-give your time?

- Is it a client you don't want to lose?
- Is it a person you feel sorry for or someone you are infatuated with?
- Are you in a relationship in which you are giving and giving and not getting what you need in return?

When you know what you are worth and act accordingly, you will receive the value and respect that you deserve.

SHIFT YOUR FOCUS
ON CHALLENGES

If you look at every challenge in your life as a way for you to grow, then life becomes less about what's actually happening to you and more about your growth and evolution as a human being. So, when you are contemplating a hardship in your life, instead of wondering why it is happening to you, change your focus to how you can best handle the hardship and where you want to be when it is over.

Seeing only the hardship keeps you stuck in a running monologue: "This is so bad…so stressful. Why is my life like this?" That's when you can shift your focus. Look for ways to handle the situation better. Creative solutions and opportunities to move in a different direction will come forth. The key is to find ways to move towards your vision instead of dredging up reasons for why you have to suffer.

YOU'LL DO IT IF IT'S IMPORTANT TO YOU

If you really want to do something, you will go out and do it. No one will have to motivate you. You will be relentless in the pursuit of a yearning desire in your heart; you will be willing to go through hell to get there. Stop judging yourself for not being more or doing more. If you want to do more, find reasons that will make you get up and do it rather than reasons to beat yourself up for not doing it.

So, if you say you want to do something but you are not doing it, it's because it really is not important to you, even though you may think it is. You might say you want to exercise more, eat healthier, keep your house cleaner, be more organized, get another job, have more money, or spend more time with your children, and so on, but if you are not doing those things, it is because other things are a higher priority, although you may not realize it or even want to admit it.

We always have the time, money, energy, and resources to do the things we truly want to do. That said, it is time to stop judging yourself for not being more or doing more. You're doing exactly what you want to do, even if it's not what's "best" for you. If you want to do more, find reasons that will make you get up and do it instead of reasons to beat yourself up for not doing it.

RUDE PEOPLE AND BAD TREATMENT

People will treat you exactly the same way you unconsciously treat your-self. Whenever someone doesn't appreciate the value of your time and it bothers you, ask yourself this: In what ways do *you* fail to appreciate the value of your own time? When you feel slighted by a cutting remark, ask yourself in what way you have been cutting yourself down.

Here is a powerful way to take control of your daily experiences: be consciously aware of the beliefs and feelings you have about yourself and then monitor them as people reflect them. As you begin to treat yourself better, this can transform your experience of how others treat you.

So, instead of getting upset about what others say or do to you, look within, and see in what way you have been doing the same thing to yourself. It may be in a different form, but open and curious introspection will show you that the manners of others always mirror the manners you show to yourself.

SUCCESS STARTS WITH YOU

You emanate a ripple effect that goes out to everyone you know, and even to those you don't know. It emanates outwards to the very edges of our universe. Inevitably, it touches many lives along the way. Fully acknowledge that you make an impact just by being alive. The moment you do, your consciousness expands, your energy shifts, and your drive to fulfill your personal goals automatically increases, leading you towards success.

Remember that your words and actions, no matter how seemingly small and insignificant, do make a real difference. When they are aligned with your heart, your purpose expands and your ability to achieve success increases, inevitably moving you towards fulfilling your inspired destiny.

AVOID UNREALISTIC EXPECTATIONS

If you enter into a relationship thinking that your partner will always support you in the way you want, never get on your nerves, always be incredibly loving and fair, and never neglect you or say a mean thing, you have an unrealistic expectation.

In any relationship, there are as many negatives as there are positives. If you can be mindful enough not to place extra pressure on your partner to deliver according to your standards and one-sided expectations, you will fare much better. Just let your partner be who he is. Make the choice to love him as he is and for what he brings to your life instead of condemning him for who he isn't and how he is not meeting your needs. This is just a reminder to be thankful for the person you are in relationship with.

It must also be said that if your partner consistently brings more negatives than positives into your life, you may want to think about why you are still with this person. Either look for a significant need your partner fulfills that you have not been appropriately thankful for—or let him go.

WHEN IT'S HARD TO FEEL GRATEFUL

It's easy to feel thankful and appreciative when things are going well. During these times, it's effortless to come up with a list of things you are grateful for. When gratitude matters the most, though, is when you feel that your life is filled with challenges—whether it's a broken heart, a work or financial crisis, a challenging child, aging parent concerns, a health issue, or losing your job. During such times, it's hard to summon up gratitude for the pain and difficulty you are experiencing.

Yet, ironically, dealing with challenges leads you to find deeper levels of strength, creativity, and understanding of yourself and your life. There is always a bigger picture to your challenges, even if it is not apparent currently. It will helpful to look back on your greatest challenges and notice how they have brought you to where you are today. If you hadn't gotten dumped, faced that health challenge, or lost that job, where would you be now?

Reflect on specific painful events in your life and see the inherent good that came from them; this will help you trust that what you are going through now also has a divine purpose. In short, to comfort yourself during these hard times, use the past as a reference to experience gratitude in your present challenges.

IT'S ABOUT YOU

Sometimes the people you complain about (you know, the ones who are in your way, stressing you out, and creating problems for you) are actually the ones who are assisting you the most. Why? Because they force you to face what in *you* is holding you back from achieving what you want.

Instead of lamenting about these irritating people and hoping they'll get run over by a truck, ask yourself what *you* need to do to get on with your life.

- Do you need to work on your security issues?
- Do you need to be more confident in your path?
- Do you need to refocus on what is really important?
- Do you need to get over the need to please others?
- Do you need to let go of judgment?
- Do you need to change who you hang out with?

- Do you need to form new habits?
- Do you just need to have another drink? J

Remember, it is not about someone else. It always is, and always will be, about you.

IF THEY HAVE IT, YOU HAVE IT

Understanding the Law of Reflection can be a great way to neutralize the polarities of resentment and infatuation and lessen the baggage of illusion we often carry. The Law of Reflection states that you have the qualities you see in others, whatever they are. So, whether you judge a quality in someone else to be "amazing" or "loathsome," until you see it within you, you will live with a perception of lack or an imbalanced view of yourself.

The power of this law lies in your willingness to honestly reflect and find within yourself the very traits you admire or resent in others.

Self-reflection is one of the most incredible tools I know of, as it not only can balance your emotions, but it can raise your consciousness and bring forth abundance. Self-reflection has the power to open your heart to love.

GREATNESS TAKES TIME

Some people fail to understand is that what seems like an overnight success may have taken many years. Truly, it is more about the journey than it is about the destination. After all, we don't listen to a song just to get to the end; we listen for the experience of the emotions it evokes as we sing along. We don't read a book just to get to the end; we immerse ourselves so we can get "lost" in the story. We don't fantasize about coming home again when we start out on a trip; we go on a trip to create memories and have new and joyful experiences. Life is no different. Your journey defines it.

As such, let that journey be one that is congruent with what is most meaningful to you, and you will find the success you are seeking. You will not only make a greater difference to more people, you will find the success and greatness you are seeking.

COMPLETE AT LEAST ONE TASK EVERY DAY

You'll feel better and more fulfilled at the end of the day if you complete at least one thing on your to-do list every day—not a *should*, but something that you actually must do. Not only will you feel better, but you also will attract more opportunities. When you complete a task, you empower your will.

Determine right this minute what that is, and commit to tying up at least one loose end. Don't leave things hanging. If what you have to do is uninspiring, focus on the positive confidence that will emerge from accomplishment. The very act of completion is a magnet for more opportunities that are aligned with your goals, dreams, and desires.

Focus on the power of accomplishment today. Commit to it by writing down *one thing* you will do today.

THOSE WHO HAVE PASSED ON ARE WITH YOU

If you are missing a loved one or a beloved pet who is no longer on this plane of existence, remember this: Each of us is far more than just our physical body, and because our spirits and souls are infinite and timeless in nature, the essence of who we are is able to interweave among and permeate all dimensions. Therefore, when you think of your loved ones who are gone, know that they too are "thinking" of you. When you see something or someone who reminds you of them, recognize it as a symbol that they are clearly showing themselves in this special form—and it's just for you.

Your thoughts, feelings, and intuition are intangible, but they are vehicles by which you can connect to those who are no longer in human form and are operating on the spiritual plane. So, although you may miss your loved one or pet, here in the physical, always remember that you are fully, deeply, and inextricably connected to them in the nonphysical. Anytime you have a memory that triggers the love you have in your heart for a departed loved one, know without a shadow of a doubt that it is they who initiated the connection.

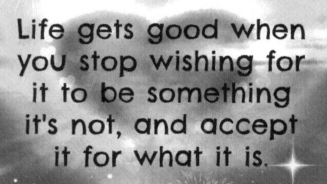

Life gets good when you stop wishing for it to be something it's not, and accept it for what it is.

HAPPINESS

yourhappinessu.com

EVERYTHING IS A MIRROR

Everything you see in others is a mirror of yourself. That's why it's much easier to love and accept others when you love and accept yourself. Focus on fully embracing all of your traits, especially the ones you don't like. Lifting the expectations and conditions you place on yourself lifts your expectations of others and the conditions you place on them.

Whenever you put someone down or get irritated when someone does or says something that you just "can't stand," it's actually because you also have the same trait in you and you either don't want to admit it, think you don't have it, want to get rid of it, suppress the expression of it and/or you judge it to be bad. So, make life easier for yourself. Instead of trying to change others, which never works, work towards accepting yourself for all that you are, and watch how it magically stops them from getting on your last nerve.

OUR CHALLENGES HAVE A PURPOSE

You will never be given a challenge or crisis that you can't handle, though while you are in the midst of it, it can feel overwhelming and bring up negative or depressing thoughts. During such times, remember that your challenges always have a purpose. They help you grow, assist you in finding your hidden power, and eventually reveal valuable gifts for you and the world around you to which you are currently blind.

In the moment, the best way to cope with your challenges is to focus on asking yourself questions like:

- What am I getting out of this (besides pain and frustration)?
- Am I seeing how much people care?
- Am I learning new things about myself that I didn't know?

- Am I developing compassion and/or am I understanding others in new ways?
- Am I meeting people, learning things, or doing things that I would never have done had I not had this challenge?

There is a divine order to and a purpose for everything that is happening in your life. The more you take the time to look and the more deeply you look, the easier it will be to let go of the mindset that your challenge is "the worst thing ever." Just as calm weather exists in the eye of a cyclone, so also can you experience peace and balance by looking for the hidden blessings in the eye of your personal crisis.

WHAT IS COMMITMENT?

Have you ever thought about what it really means when someone says they are committed to you (or to your project, your goals, your vision, etc.)? You may think someone is committed to you, but in reality, they are actually committed to what is most important to them. As human beings, we all make decisions based on what we feel is to our greatest advantage. Even if someone says they are committed to you, they are actually only committed because it fulfills what is most important to them.

For example, if someone says that, by committing to you, they are "sacrificing" their time, energy (or whatever) for you, they are actually doing it for themselves, whether or not they realize it. It may be that showing loyalty or not letting you down is more important to them than their own happiness. Either way, people act upon what fulfills them the most.

So, if you want someone to stick to their commitments to you, then you need to understand what is important to them and make sure there are more advantages and rewards to them because of their commitment to you. If not, they are likely to waiver and move towards a path they perceive as being more advantageous, letting you down in the process.

THE GIFT OF LIFE

Health challenges that threaten to shorten our time on earth often serve to wake us up and make us face any realities that we have been ignoring. In other words, when an injury or disease shows up, we are forced to get immediately present with what is most important. That is the gift of life that each of us has been given. For many of us, it's not until we are diagnosed with something life-threatening that we truly begin to live and appreciate life for what it is.

As the Dalai Lama said, "We live as though we are never going to die, and die without having ever really lived." Today, cherish the gift of life. What is truly important? Could it be that what it all boils down to is to simply appreciate the life you've been given…and to give and receive love?

MONEY IS YOUR FRIEND

People often wonder why they don't have money, even though they love it and say they want more of it. What they really love is what money can buy. That's why they spend their money on consumables, liabilities, and things that depreciate. Soon, they look around and wonder why they still don't have any money.

I've found that many people treat money like they do relationships they don't care about. They stop paying attention to it and start using it for what it's good for. Think about it this way, if you always used your friend to get what you wanted, that friend would not hang around you for long, right? In the same way, money leaves the hands of those who use it for personal gain.

The bottom line is this: If you want to have more money, treat it like you would your best friend. Put your energy and focus on saving it, investing in it, appreciating it, and keeping it near. If you don't want to put that kind of energy into it, then fully enjoy what money can buy you! And don't keep asking why you don't have any.

Love Yourself

If you're 100% in...
YOU WIN

Yay!

HAPPINESS
YourHappinessU.com

BALANCE YOUR RESENTMENT

Have you noticed that when you feel resentful towards someone, you focus on all the negatives of their attitudes or behaviors that don't match up with your expectations of them? Resentment is a form of internal anger that you grab onto when someone doesn't act in a way that you think they *should*. When you feel resentful towards someone, you focus on the negatives, right? When you are infatuated with someone, you focus on the positives and overlook the negatives, isn't that true? Neither viewpoint is healthy.

In the case of resentment, the key is to balance out your perspective by searching for the underlying positives to the person or situation you resent. You can ask yourself:

- How is this person's behavior helping me?
- What is the person or situation helping me to become aware of?
- Do I need to learn to speak up?

- Do I need to set more realistic expectations?
- Do I need to stop giving so much and learn to value my time and energy more?

Ultimately, the person you are resenting is helping you to grow and get clearer. When you can find the positive aspect of it, you can minimize and ultimately "cure" the resentment.

THE UNIVERSE BEHAVES AS WE DO

We are built on universal principles, and the universe behaves as we do, but on a grander scale. If you gave someone a gift and they just glanced at it and tossed it aside without thanks, would you be inclined to give them another gift? Of course not, and the universe responds in the same manner. The universe bestows its gifts where they are most appreciated.

If you are not thankful and appreciative for what you have in your life now, why would the universe give you more? The more appreciative you are today, the more you will have to appreciate tomorrow.

Here is a simple tip for experiencing gratitude: Write thank you letters. Sometimes our best thoughts and ideas are those we do not try to edit, so let the message you write come to you in the moment. There is no need for the words to make sense to anyone except the person for whom it is intended.

WHAT *HAVE* YOU ACCOMPLISHED?

Today, make an effort to notice what you *are* accomplishing. Not what you thought you wanted to get done, but what you actually did. Stop judging yourself; it only holds you back and wastes your energy; it serves no purpose except to make you feel bad. Shift your focus! I know it's natural to focus on what you didn't do and beat yourself up for not doing it, but don't.

Instead, acknowledge what you *are* getting done. This will reduce your inner conflict, dissipate your resistance, and accelerate your pace towards achievement. Give yourself permission to treat yourself with more love and understanding. You'll feel better and get more done—I promise.

HOW TO BE AUTHENTIC

We all say we want to be authentic. We are happiest, most centered, and ultimately most fulfilled when we can just be ourselves. And yet, we put on these social masks that project an identity that is not true to who we really are inside. Why do we do this?

When we think that someone is more important or better than us in some way, it reduces our perception of our own value, so we put on a mask of inferiority when interacting with them. On the other hand, if we judge someone as lacking in some way, we put on a mask of superiority when interacting with them. We decide what mask to wear based on what we think about ourselves and what we think about the person with whom we are engaged.

The masks we wear give others the impression of someone who is not really who we seem to be, and this is what separates us from our authenticity. The more masks you wear, the less comfortable you are with who you are, and the less authentically you live your life.

Learning how to be authentic is a process. To start, be honest about who you are and what you love to do, and don't judge it. Then, start to work towards living your life according to what is truly most important to *you*—not what is most important to others. Living authentically is the key to your success and ultimate fulfillment. When you put on a mask, you weaken yourself. Remember, no persona or mask can possibly compete with the true and amazing you! You are perfect exactly the way you are. The moment you embrace this, nothing will be able to stop you from your ultimate goals.

KNOW WHERE YOU ARE HEADED

If you are a leader—owner, manager, supervisor, team captain—get clear on your inspiration, vision, mission, and goals for your team. Know where you are headed, and how you will get there. The clearer you are, the fewer obstacles you will face as a team, and the more spirit, talent, and power you will awaken in those whom you lead.

When your words originate from the depth of your being and are congruent with providing a loving service to others, you will inspire enthusiasm and be a leader that your team will gladly follow. Your degree of dedication to leadership, your clarity, and your ability to communicate your innermost vision will be directly proportionate to the rate at which you achieve success.

TAKE ACTION ON INSPIRATION

When you take action on things that inspire you rather than get distracted by things that take you away from your goals, you feel alive, productive, and purposeful. To move in this direction consistently, be aware of who you surround yourself with and the content of your conversations. There are those who live intentionally and are meaningful and productive to communicate with. Others just want to take up your time with small talk.

Just remember this: Small talk leads to a small vision and small gains. Although there are times you cannot avoid it, don't let small talk and people who have less on their plate than you do, take over your life. Learn to say no to idle chatter and set yourself free to move towards the vast potential of your greatest dreams by spending time speaking with people who share your vision. "Big" talk leads to big visions and big gains.

BE AWARE OF YOUR SELF-TALK

We all talk to ourselves. Sometimes this self-talk is positive and builds us up, and other times it's negative and brings us down. It's important to remember that words are power that runs through your mind and help you create the reality in which you experience life. Use your self-talk to help you hone in on, and manifest what is most important to you. Words of affirmation can help when you feel you are getting off-track. Here are a few of my favorites that I say daily:

- Everything I desire is completely within my reach.
- How I see things is in my mind and in my control.
- I set up realistic expectations of myself and others in every circumstance.
- All my challenges become my stepping stones to new opportunities.

- I create financial abundance by doing what I love to do.
- Everything I am doing or am not doing is serving a beneficial purpose.

IT'S ABOUT YOU, AND IT'S ABOUT LOVE

Today, make it a point to affirm that you are an incredible human being, contributing in your own unique way, and know that you are an important part of this world. After all, if you didn't exist, the world would not be the same. You make an inspiring difference to so many. The same goes for everyone else you know, as well as for the people you don't know. Everyone makes a difference.

Therefore, it's important to find balance in each day. As you practice doing this, you will realize that right smack in the middle, between the positive and negative emotions you feel, between the good and the bad, and between your infatuation with others and resentment of others is the core of the human experience —and it is simply about love.

Here's my point: Instead of wishing for a life filled with "perfect" partners, clients, friends, spouses, children, parents, coworkers, and so on, appreciate everyone in your life for what they bring to you, for no matter what they do or don't do, they are teaching you about love.

EVERYTHING HAS TWO SIDES

We live in a two-sided world. Everything we experience has two sides to it. You are two-sided. Events are two-sided. Everything from the micro to the macro has duality. Life is where we experience the duality and have the opportunity to understand that complementary opposites exist at every level of our being and in life itself. You can't understand *happy* without *sad*. Life cannot be up without any downs. You cannot be only nice and never mean. There is no growth without breakdown, and neither can there be positive without negative.

The sooner you recognize that there is no such thing as a one-sided, all-positive life, the happier you will be. If you still insist on pursuing an all-positive life in a dualistic world – you will inevitably lead yourself into unrealistic expectations, disappointments, and ultimately, depression. Happiness occurs when you stop expecting life to be something it's not and accept it for what it is. Accept the not-so-positive things in your life and notice how balanced you become.

YOUR WHOLE LIFE HAS PREPARED YOU FOR WHAT LIES AHEAD.

HAPPINESS

YourHappinessU.com

THE CYCLES OF LIFE

In business, just as in life, there are natural cycles. When things are going great and you have good cash flow, you feel upbeat and optimistic. You may even feel as though you've conquered the world! It's natural in this "up" cycle to relax and stop doing the things that brought you there. When your working capital is low or non-existent, you feel down and impatient for success. During the low phase of the cycle, we become creative and act purposefully, just as we did when we first started our business. Business is a cycle, and low-money cycles drive us to create and spurn new action.

To avoid extreme highs and lows, discipline yourself to balance your mindset consistently. When things are going well, focus on areas in which you can do better. When things are not going so well, focus on what you *are* doing that's good.

LOST FULFILLMENT IS A REASON FOR CHANGE

Looking back to the past, do you find that either a crisis or extreme desperation forced you to make a major change in your life? We are willing to go through the pain and uncertainty involved in making changes only when we reach the point where we are no longer fulfilled by what we are doing or by the people with whom we are interacting, When the pain of staying in the same place overrides the pain involved in taking action, when uncertainty about the future no longer matters as much as the certainty of the present, you will make a change. In fact, you are ripe for change if you no longer feel fulfilled by what you are doing, lack energy, and feel uninspired every day. What do you need? Is it a change of situation or a change in attitude that you need? Either one may be exactly what you need.

HAPPINESS IS NOT A MOOD

Happiness is a natural way to feel. You can naturally begin to feel happier. All you have to do is:

- Give up your judgments of yourself and others.
- Stop wishing that life will give you only positive experiences ('cause it won't).
- Take the time to know who you are.

Remember, life was not made to be easy; it was meant to help us grow. The easier you want your life to be, the harder it will seem to be. Accept life as it is and others as they are, and happiness will quite naturally accompany you along your journey.

YOUR EMOTIONS AND YOUR WEALTH ARE LINKED

If you can't control your emotions, how do you expect to control your wealth? To illustrate my point, I want you to imagine that you just lost half your life's savings due to a sharp drop in the stock market. It is likely that you would feel emotionally down about it. Now, imagine that you just won the largest jackpot ever in Las Vegas. Can you imagine how emotionally *up* you would feel?

This same principle works in reverse—as your emotions fluctuate, your ability to accumulate wealth fluctuates. If you want to accumulate wealth, create balanced and sound strategies that override your emotions. You make money from your strategies, not from your emotions.

This is what Warren Buffet meant when he said, "Until you can manage your emotions, don't expect to manage money."

LOOK FOR WHAT YOU'VE BEEN BLIND TO

Have you ever noticed that when you resent someone, you can't help but notice everything about them that you don't like? Have you also noticed that some part of you thinks you are better than them? Likewise, when you are infatuated with someone, have you noticed that you seem to like everything about them? At the same time, you compare yourself to them unfavorably because you think that person has something that you don't. In reality, neither of these people is better or worse than you. What is happening is that your perceptions are influencing your emotions.

If you allow your emotions and perceptions to run you, you will get thrown off-balance. Emotions need to be balanced with a solid strategy.

If you are in the position of either resenting or idealizing someone, make it a point to look for what you are not seeing. Find the upsides of the person you resent and notice the downsides of the person with whom

132

you are infatuated. You have the ability to control how you feel. Take an honest look at what you are blind to in others, and you will see the balance that is inherent in every person and every situation.

A balanced mind is the key to an open heart.

HAPPINESS
YourHappinessU.com

WHAT IS OF TRUE VALUE TO YOU?

Identify what is truly the most valuable to you and let go of your low priorities. When you know what you want, give yourself permission to make the time for it. Concentrate on it, and you will begin to master your life. Remember, when you engage in what is truly meaningful to you, you make a difference. You build momentum and feel more inspired. This leads to more gratitude, which is a catalyst to getting more of what you want in life.

At the end of your life, I'm sure you want to be able to say that you did everything you could with everything you were given. You are an extraordinary human being. You have what it takes to be successful by doing what is meaningful and valuable to you. Make this your focus, and give yourself permission to shine.

WHO DO YOU HANG AROUND WITH?

Are you associating with people who assist you by holding you accountable for the vision you have for your life, or do you hang out with people who drag you down? You will be most successful when you surround yourself with people who inspire you and when you engage information resources that expand you. Stop doing things that are low on your list of priorities. Otherwise, you'll be constantly frustrated and beat yourself up for not being able to move towards that which you most desire.

Prioritize every aspect of your life, do what you are inspired to do, and delegate the rest. Otherwise, you'll be constantly frustrated and beat yourself up for not being able to move towards what you most desire. I've learned that the best way to get where I want to go is to focus on the 25 percent of my to-do list that gives back 75 percent of my desired results.

REFLECTION IS ALL YOU NEED

When I am feeling down, I know that if I take the time to reflect upon my life, it will help me feel better. I look for evidence that literally everything I have ever experienced from the day I was born, whether I liked it or not, has served me to perfection and added infinite value to my life. Even the disappointments, low points, shattered dreams, and betrayals have helped me to grow in ways that have led me to my greatest joys and accomplishments.

It is the same for you. Every positive and negative experience has guided you and shaped your path. When you really "get" that all that has happened has led you to where you are today, it's almost impossible not to feel humbled by the intelligence that governs this universe and be blown away by the divine order of synchronicities that bring the people, circumstances, and situations to you in just the way you need so you can grow and evolve.

So, if you are going through something particularly challenging right now, just keep breathing, stay strong, and trust that there is a bigger picture. Affirm in your heart that one day you will most certainly gain from what you are experiencing. So, hang in there. We are all in this life together.

CHOICES AND THE VIRTUAL LIST IN YOUR HEAD

Everything in life is up to you and everything is a choice. When you reach a crossroads or a crisis, or when you have a moment of uncertainty, is there a virtual list inside your head that you read and reread and rely on to make a decision? Is it the one that features obstacles, defects, criticism, the unfairness of life, and all the challenges?

How about this: Turn it over and read the list on the flipside, which highlights amazing possibilities yet to unfold, supportive friends and loved ones along the way, and all the synchronicities that put you in the right place at the right time to be exactly where you are today.

Remember, at every juncture, you have a choice. Rely on the side of your virtual list that represents your positive potential, and the decision you make will take you to where you can shine in unprecedented ways. It's always your choice, and it's always up to you.

YOUR PERSONAL IDEALS AND REALITY

We have these ideas about *who* we think we should be and *where* we think we should be in life. Sounds fine, but when we perceive that we are falling short, we beat ourselves up for not being better or further along than we are. Anytime you measure your progress according to one standard, you are ignoring the reality of life, because there are two sides to everything. Be thankful for what is or you will lose touch with the present moment.

When you live in the reality of how things really are, you will make much faster progress toward your ultimate vision and highest aspirations.

To expand your spirit and feel whole, you need to water the seed of the positive daily. Remember, it's not about where you *are not;* it's about where you *are*. In what areas are you in the right place, living the right life?

THE GIFT OF GROWTH

The challenges you
are going through
today will one day
be a memory.

#lifeistough
#gottakeepgoing
#focusonthegift

YourHappinessU.com

LIFE DOESN'T ALWAYS GO OUR WAY

At times, it's easy to wonder why life doesn't always go the way you want. Why don't others do what you want them to? Why do you get caught up in these complex situations in which you feel trapped? Why does life feel so hard sometimes?

Here is one way to understand it: The universe is here to teach you to grow and to evolve and to find your deepest power and purpose.

The expectation that life should be easier and should have more positives than negatives is unrealistic. Thinking that way sets you up to experience more negativity and feel more pain. Why is that? Because life is trying to show you that there is a balance.

We grow on the edge of challenge and support. So, today, create balance by looking for the good that is coming out of your current challenge. See it for the catalyst it is. See the new direction your life is taking because of it. Truly, everything happens for a reason. Find those reasons and you can begin moving towards the lighted path of a new reality that is filled with peace, joy, and personal power.

APPRECIATION OPENS YOU UP TO OPPORTUNITY

It's easy at times to feel like you need to be a more perfect version of yourself instead of appreciating yourself for who you really are. However, it is important to know that when you look at yourself this way, you are closing down your life to opportunity. From now on, instead of looking at your supposed deficits, make it a point to acknowledge your assets and the value you bring to the world. When you do this, you automatically will receive more blessings than ever before.

Your conscious focus has the power to alter the course of your life.

So, embrace your true and radiant self and give yourself permission to shine like the sun in a clear-blue sky. You can transform your life simply by appreciating yourself for the incredible person you are instead of depreciating yourself for not being someone you aren't. Your most important relationship is the one you have with yourself.

ACCEPT YOURSELF AS YOU ARE

You probably are familiar with the Law of Attraction. Well, there are many universal laws, and one of my favorites is the Law of Relativity. It states that nothing is good, bad, big, or small until you compare it to something else. So, everything in your life just *is*—until you start comparing it, and nothing in life has any meaning except for the meaning you give it. Today, remember the Law of Relativity: Accept yourself as you are and accept others as they are.

Whenever you are feeling "less than" or even "more than," stop comparing yourself to a person or an ideal in your head. Everything is relative at any given moment. Don't waste time or energy thinking that you should have done more, been more, or be further along.

NO ONE ELSE'S OPINION IS MORE IMPORTANT THAN YOURS

Have you ever noticed that you lose your sense of self and step out of your power when you meet someone whom you perceive as being "better" than you are in some way? On the other hand, if you think that person doesn't have as much physical beauty, or status, or attributes you consider important, you don't care what they think of you, and it's easy to stay strong. When you think someone else's opinion is more important than yours, you feel the pain of rejection. You minimize yourself relative to them and start sacrificing your own needs and desires to please them.

Don't lose yourself in trying to please people you think are more important than you. Remember, you are just as important. Every day you wake up, you can know with certainty that you are a magnificent being who is not to be minimized. Honor your true and radiant self.

WHY IS MY LIFE LIKE THIS?

Have you ever thought, "My life is not supposed to be like this! Why is this happening to me?"

It's natural to think this way during challenging times, and it is easy to get stuck in this mindset. It's important and necessary to vent, to share, and to seek understanding, but remember not to get all wrapped up in your head about how your life is "supposed" to be. If you do, you'll miss the beauty in how your life actually is.

Also, when the reality of your life doesn't match the perfect picture you see in your head, there's a reason.

Quite simply, you are not seeing what life is trying to show you. Right now, take a moment to look for a few very specific situations in your life that you love, ones that wouldn't be there if your life really matched the perfect picture. Do you wish your ex never existed in your life? Without him or her, you wouldn't have your children. Do you wish you had more meaningful work? But if you didn't have this job, you would never have met some great co-workers who have become life-long friends. The beauty of life is always there when we take the time to look for it. Once you can accept this, it's much easier to move forward towards your heart-centered visions.

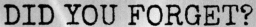

DID YOU FORGET?
(RE: The people in your life)

You are here to
love them.

Not fix them.

YourHappinessU.com

IT'S ALL ABOUT HOW YOU SEE IT

If you feel your life is filled with problems and challenges these days, if you feel stuck in some situation, remember the polarity of life. We can be happy and sad, mean and nice, and even horrible and wonderful all in the same moment. It's the same with a problem—it cannot exist without a solution. A challenge cannot exist without a corresponding benefit, and you cannot experience a crisis that does not contain a hidden blessing.

So, what's going on does not matter as much as your perception of what's going on and what you choose to do about it. The reality is, a lot of movement is going on when you feel stuck, however it is movement back into the mindset of being stuck, and it happens repeatedly.

Today, instead of affirming how stuck you feel, look for opportunities to affirm ways in which your problem is leading you to explore new avenues of thought and growth. Pave your own way out. The world will not change for you. Nothing will change until you do.

YOUR LIFE IS AN OPPORTUNITY

Have you ever thought of your life as an opportunity to do things your way? This does not mean doing things the way you were raised or the way someone else thinks you should do them—and it definitely does not mean the way others would do them. As you begin to accept that you are the master of your life, your corresponding choices unlock inner freedom and joy so that your true expression of who you are can emerge in powerful and magnificent ways.

Remain true to your spirit each day by humbly speaking your truth and setting the intent to live your life in an unprecedented way. Drop *should* and *shouldn't* from your vocabulary. Instead, ask yourself, "What is right for me?" From there, move forward with grace and love into the fullest expression of who you are. Your life is waiting for you to make it yours.

BE SELF-CENTERED

The life you have is *your* life, so give yourself permission to live it fully. Sometimes we lose our center and get caught up in doing what others or society think is best for us. It's wise to remind yourself often that you are a unique individual, that you have only one life to live, and that what is "right" is what is truly important to you

Practice being self-centered, not in an egotistical way, but in a way that serves your life best. Only from a place of centeredness can you make the best decisions for yourself, reach your goals, and be of greatest service to others. Is it time for you to stop betraying yourself to please others? If you have been operating off-center these days, and losing energy and feeling uninspired, then it is time to re-center.

LIFE IS SOMETIMES UNEXPLAINABLE

Life is filled with situations and circumstances that are unexplainable. Many times, things that happen bring joy to our hearts, and other times, they bring deep pain. If you are in a difficult situation and wonder how you can get through another moment, let alone another day, stop resisting what you can't change. I know it's hard to stop, but the more you resist, the longer your bad feelings will persist.

Instead, work towards embracing *what is* and trust that, however messed up things seem and no matter who or what caused it, there is a divine order at play in your life. Once you take steps towards accepting this and see that *everything* in your life is here to serve you and support you in your growth, you begin to heal. You can only move forward when you stop wishing your life was something it isn't and embrace it for what it is.

FEEL JOY IN THE MIDST OF PAIN

When does the pain of life end? When does the joy of life begin? Is it even possible to feel joy in the midst of pain? Or do you just wait patiently for joy to emerge, if ever? Sometimes, life really stretches our trust in the possibility that we can be truly happy from within, especially in light of all the personal complexities, negative thoughts, and challenges that so easily weigh us down. I have found that life is never going to be what I want it to be. It is going to be what it is, and it's up to me to find the happiness within *what is.*

If we look, the light is always there, although sometimes, we just want to give up the search for it. You may put a smile on the outside, but how you really feel on the inside is what counts. Take a moment to look within. What exists in your life that can begin to illuminate the shadows in your heart? It is there. You just have to look for it. Once you find it, focus on it. Remember, no one can change your life except you.

YOU DON'T NEED PERMISSION TO GROW.

YOU ARE THE AUTHORITY OF YOUR LIFE.

YourHappinessU.com

P.S. NOT EVERYONE WILL AGREE AND THAT'S OKAY.

THE LAW OF CAUSE AND EFFECT

A very important universal law is the Law of Cause and Effect, which states that every cause (action) has an effect, and every effect becomes the cause for something else. The universe is always in motion, always progressing and evolving through a chain of events, and for every action you initiate, there is an equal energetic effect.

This means that when you use your thoughts, actions, and feelings with strong intention, what you create not only goes out to others in the same manner but is also returned to you. The same goes for when you use lower or more negative energies to create. The universe always returns what you have initiated. There are no coincidences, only divine synchronicities, and everything you experience over time is in direct proportion to the causes you set into motion.

MANIFEST WHAT YOU WANT

When you feel afraid, have you noticed it's often because you think you'll lose what you have or won't get what you want? The next time one of these two fears comes up for you, remember that your fear is not about loss; it's about how you would feel if you were to experience loss or not get what you want.

It is perfectly safe to feel your feelings, whatever they are, so the next time you feel afraid, allow yourself to feel what you are afraid of feeling, just for a moment. Breathe deeply, and consciously accept the feeling. Having embraced and accepted your unwanted feelings, you are now free to feel the welcome feelings that come with getting what you want. Now, you have control over attracting what you want into your life, instead. You are a powerful manifestor. Manifest what you want, not what you are afraid of!

ACCEPTING THINGS FOR WHAT THEY ARE

Are there areas of your life in which things are not exactly working out the way you imagined they would? Did you have a different vision of how you wanted things to unfold? Depending on what the issue is, this kind of disappointment can be both difficult and emotional, especially when it comes to matters of the heart, your health, friendships, and work. How can you push through it? How do you know when to let go?

Direct your attention away from the past (the way things were) and the future (fear that it's not going to be what you want) and focus instead on the present. Soon, you will experience greater ease. This means neither pushing through nor trying to let go, but instead focusing on accepting the situation for what it is. There is always a gift in every challenge, and as hard as it is, look towards the bigger picture and trust that everything is going to be okay. It is only from this place of balance that you can move towards a new, more positive reality.

THERE IS A WAY OUT

Are you feeling pulled apart in some way? Are things not going as smoothly as you would like, or are you feeling more emotional than usual? Perhaps you aren't as efficient as you'd like to be, or you aren't meeting your personal expectations of yourself and are feeling down. In all such cases, do your best to stop resisting what is, and accept that things are the way they are for a reason.

Expand beyond what you perceive is possible for yourself and your life. No matter how complex and challenging your situation, there is a way to move through it, and the reality that you have created for yourself has to change in order for you to change. Focus on the path out, not on the obstacles you are currently facing.

HAPPINESS IS NOT JUST ABOUT BEING POSITIVE

Happiness comes from being centered and balanced internally; it's not just feeling positive about everything all the time. In fact, it is not natural to be constantly "up" and positive, and anytime you think you *should* be, you'll end up getting down on yourself for it, causing instability in your emotional and mental state.

Embrace both sides of yourself, the positive and the negative aspects of your life and your circumstances, and this will give you access to a sense of balance and centeredness. If you equate happiness with feeling only positive and good, you will never be happy. Change your mindset about this one thing, and you will feel less polar and more stable, and your sense of inner balance will emerge stronger than ever.

THE PROCRASTINATOR'S MANTRA

"I always get done what
I need to get done when
the time is right.

I am in the right place,
at the right time, doing
the right thing."

#StopBeatingMyselfUp
#FeelsGoodToSayThis

YourHappinessU.com

THE EXTREMES IN LIFE

At various times in our lives, extremes tend to show up more than ever. On one hand, you may be experiencing unprecedented joys, while on the other hand, you may be having to navigate challenging complexities. If this is you right now, remind yourself often that all is in divine order. Everything is happening simply so that you can find your truth, bring forth your power, and set your sights on new horizons.

Try to find meaning in your challenges so that they will serve as fuel for your inspiration. Remember, you create your future every moment of every day. Break the boundaries of all you have ever known and believed. Feel your pains deeply as you fully embrace your challenges, and just as day follows night, your life will soon take new flight as a greater and even more meaningful purpose emerges.

VALUE OTHERS TO INCREASE YOUR VALUE

When is the last time you said, "How are you?" to someone and genuinely cared about their answer? Make it a point to value someone everyday by showing a heartfelt interest in their response. It won't take much more of your time. All it really requires is more awareness. Sometimes, we get so caught up with ourselves that we forget to take the time to be present with others.

What happens when you do this? That person feels valued, and when you offer value, you increase your value to others. Amazing synchronicities come forth, and things of value move toward you more rapidly. Use the Law of Attraction to help yourself and others at the same time. It's a genuine win-win.

WHERE DO YOU WANT TO BE?

It's natural to resist challenges due to fear of change. Anytime you are in a situation where you see that your life is about to take a different turn, it's helpful to think back to past times of difficulty. Focus on how, now, in retrospect, those shifts have served you well and led you to where you are today. If you feel that certain things in your life are a bit complex in the present moment and are not sure how they will manifest, just focus on where you want to be, rather than fear where things are headed.

Take this opportunity to move yourself to a new level of power with a different way of thinking. Don't think as much about tangible or measurable goals; focus on how you want to feel about who you are and the choices you have made. Remember, there is a hidden order to everything, and everything is going to unfold perfectly. Life is synchronous. Everything that is happening in your life is there to help you be your best self and live your fullest life. Trust the wisdom of your heart.

WHAT YOU THINK ABOUT, YOU BRING ABOUT

It really is true that what you think about, you bring about. If you spend today dwelling on how challenging your life is, how tired you are of your job, how irritated you are with your relationships, and how little money you have, the universe will respond by mirroring your thoughts, and these challenges will feel heavier than ever.

Take the time right now to consider how this heaviness is also making your life lighter. Is your boring job helping you pay your bills? Is your irritating relationship providing you security? Is your lack of funds causing you to think seriously about what you want in life?

I've found the key to opening new doors of opportunity: Do not wait for life to change for the better; see your life as better, now. The moment you embrace what you "hate," peace will show up in your heart and new opportunities will show up in your life.

It's never too late to make the decision to make something happen for yourself.

HAPPINESS

YourHappinessU.com

YOU'LL FEEL BETTER IF YOU DO THIS

We all want to be appreciated. We want to be appreciated for who we are, for what we do, for our contributions, for our presence, for our ideas, and for everything we bring to the table of life. Do you agree?

Remember this during your interactions with others, even if they are not doing what you want, acting the way your want, or giving you what you want. What you say and what you focus on will make a positive difference. She didn't do what you want? Thank her for her effort or time. He can't seem to be on time? Thank him for his presence. The key is to find something to appreciate.

I know that when I feel appreciated, I feel valued; and in turn, I get inspired to appreciate others. Today, think of someone to whom you can extend a word or gesture of appreciation.

NOT ENOUGH TIME AND MONEY

Time, money, and value are all tied together. If you don't value your time and money, others will gladly value it and decide for you how you should use it. For example, if you don't know how you want to spend your money, someone will sell you something they want you to buy. If you are not certain what you want to do with your time, someone will get you to do something they want you to do.

It all comes down to this: If you don't value yourself, no one else will.

So, at the end of the day, month, or year, if you are bankrupt of time and money, build up your self-value. This is how to build up your bank account. Then, you'll have more time to enjoy spending your money the way you want to.

PEOPLE CLUTTER: IS THERE SUCH A THING?

The people in your life tangibly affect you and your growth; in fact, they can inhibit or enhance the opportunities that come to you. They either support you in a positive way and help you maintain your balance, or they drain you of your life force. Sometimes, you may forget you have a choice as to whom you associate with or how much you allow people's negativity to impact you.

From time to time, it's wise to look through your inventory of "people energy" to determine if you have people clutter. People clutter is anyone who is draining you or distracting you from your goals.

Is it time to let go of some people in your life? If you can't, it is time to change your attitude about them and stop using them as an excuse?

UGH! "NEGATIVE" PEOPLE ARE DRIVING ME NUTS!

The more you judge certain people in your life as "negative," and the more you judge negativity as "bad," the more their negativity will bother you. Think about it: As you focus on their negativity, contrasting it with your perceived "positivity" and feeling "righteous" (because you are so positive), the harder it is to just get on with your day. Also, in the midst of all this attention to their perceived shortcomings, you forget that you are also being and doing the very thing that bothers you about them.

Yes, other people's negativity absolutely exists, but the reason it irritates you is because you have an incomplete view of the purpose of negativity and the balance it brings to your life. Often we think that being positive is *right* and *perfect,* when in fact negativity and negative people bring balance to the whole. While they may never change, you can. If you can change your perspective to see how others' negativity plays a vital and necessary role in your life and has benefited you in some way, their negativity won't bother you as much.

Gratitude for a person's negativity can arise the moment you realize that there exists in this relationship dynamic an underlying balance of a positive for each negative. Keep your expectations of others realistic, and don't let their negativity bring you down. I know it's hard, but accept negative people for who they are, see how they have helped you, and move forward in your life.

ARE YOU PERFECT—OR NOT?

How often have you heard people use the expression, "Nobody's perfect?" It's a statement that many accept as truth, but is it really true? People usually think of perfection as one-sided and give it a one-sided definition, such as positive, good, happy, kind, and so forth. The reality is that life and people are not one-sided. Life is not always positive, good, happy, and kind, and neither are people.

If your idea of *perfect* is being kind, then whenever you are mean to someone, you compare yourself to an impossible, one-sided ideal. Instead of accepting yourself as the two-sided being that you are, you continually beat yourself up when you demonstrate the opposite, "negative" trait. You will never be able to fulfill the unrealistic expectations of perfection, because it is not in your nature to be one-sided.

The truth is, each one of us is perfect exactly as we are. You are perfect exactly as you are. The word *perfect* actually means *complete in its nature.* By nature, human beings have all traits within them, both the positive qualities and their opposites. Also, the dynamics of the world and the universe indisputably exist on a foundation of complementary opposites. Therefore, the only way to be perfect is to see perfection as two-sided. This makes every person, you included, a work of perfection.

I am Happy.

HAPPINESS
YourHappinessU.com

ABOUT THE AUTHOR

Alice Inoue is the founder and Chief Happiness Officer of Happiness University. An expert life guide, she has helped thousands of people gain clarity about their lives. Over the last fifteen years or so, she pioneered her own unique way to help others live more empowered lives. Her determination, inspiration, and success have led her to make countless appearances on radio and television as a life guide and happiness expert, and she has been prominently featured by all major publications in Hawaii, such as *Midweek, Hawaii Business Magazine, Pacific Business News,* the *Star-Advertiser* and more. In 2013, she was featured nationally on Lifetime Television's morning show, where she was interviewed about her book on happiness.

Alice has written five national award-winning books: *Be Happy! It's Your Choice, A Loving Guide to These Shifting Times, Feng Shui Your Life! Just Ask Alice,* and *Destination Happiness* all focused on life wisdom, self-growth, and happiness. *Mindful Moments* is her sixth book, a compilation of her columns that appear in the popular Hawaii publication *MidWeek,* titled "A Mindful Moment." In addition, her award-winning, weekly column that offers pertinent life guidance, "Go Ask Alice," which appears in the Sunday Star-Advertiser

Alice is the corporate presenter and primary teacher for Happiness U, a business that helps both companies and individuals develop positive mindsets in order to live more inspired private and professional lives. Find out more at: www.yourhappinessu.com